baie

W9-AOR-030

How Is
Cotton Candy Made?

by Grace Hansen

Abdo Kids Jumbo is an Imprint of Abdo Kids
abdobooks.com

abdobooks.com

Published by Abdo Kids, a division of ABDO, P.O. Box 398166, Minneapolis, Minnesota 55439.
Copyright © 2019 by Abdo Consulting Group, Inc. International copyrights reserved in all countries.
No part of this book may be reproduced in any form without written permission from the publisher.
Abdo Kids Jumbo™ is a trademark and logo of Abdo Kids.

102018

012019

THIS BOOK CONTAINS
RECYCLED MATERIALS

Photo Credits: Getty Images, iStock, Shutterstock

Production Contributors: Teddy Borth, Jennie Forsberg, Grace Hansen

Design Contributors: Dorothy Toth, Laura Mitchell

Library of Congress Control Number: 2018945974

Publisher's Cataloging-in-Publication Data

Names: Hansen, Grace, author.
Title: How is cotton candy made? / by Grace Hansen.
Description: Minneapolis, Minnesota : Abdo Kids, 2019 | Series: How is it made?
    Includes glossary, index and online resources (page 24).
Identifiers: ISBN 9781532181931 (lib. bdg.) | ISBN 9781532182914 (ebook) |
    ISBN 9781532183409 (Read-to-me ebook)
Subjects: LCSH: Candy--Juvenile literature. | Manufacturing processes--Juvenile
    literature. | Candy industry--Juvenile literature.
Classification: DDC 641.853--dc23

Table of Contents

Sweet Beginnings

Cotton candy is made up of
one ingredient, and that's sugar!
Sugar can be made from plants
like sugar cane and sugar beets.

5

The plants are **harvested** and sent to a processing plant. First, they are washed well. Then they are cut into small pieces.

Making Sugar

The pieces are put into large boilers. The hot water helps release the **elements** from the plants into the water. Those elements are what will help make the sugar.

9

The sweetened water is separated from the plant pieces. The water is cleaned and **filtered**. Then it is sent through more boilers.

The process of boiling removes a lot of the water, leaving a sweet syrup behind. The syrup is dark brown in color. It is then boiled under low pressure. This process forms crystals in the liquid.

A machine spins the crystals out of the liquid. What's left is pure sugar! Color and flavoring is added to the sugar.

Making Cotton Candy

The sugar is poured into a special machine with a heater. It heats the sugar above 375 °F (191 °C). This melts the sugar into a liquid.

The machine spins, forcing

the liquid through tiny holes.

The sugar cools down quickly.

This makes sweet threads.

A small stick collects the threads. And a fluffy batch of yummy cotton candy is ready to eat!

More Facts

- Cotton candy was originally called "Fairy Floss."

- Machine-spun cotton candy was invented in 1897 by William Morrison and John C. Wharton. The inventors were an unlikely pair! Wharton was a confectioner and Morrison was a dentist.

- Food coloring is added to the sugar to give cotton candy its fun colors!

Glossary

element – one of the parts of which something is made up.

filter – to go through a filter so that solids can be removed from a liquid.

harvest – the gathering of ripe crops.

Index

Abdo Kids ONLINE
FREE! ONLINE MULTIMEDIA RESOURCES

Visit **abdokids.com** and use this code to access crafts, games, videos, and more!

Abdo Kids Code:
HHK1931